LIT Y

# Germany

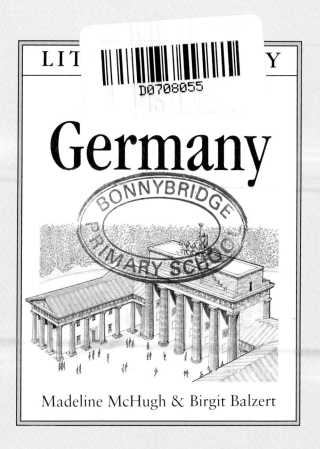

Madeline McHugh & Birgit Balzert

Kingfisher Books

# Contents

# Welcome to Germany

The tour bus pulls up in the sleepy square of a southern village. All around, high mountains look down on a cluster of neat wooden houses, each built with a steep roof to carry heavy winter snows. But this is only one small corner of a big country. There's far more yet to explore – as you'll soon see.

# The heart of Europe

Germany lies right in the very middle of Europe. To the south it rises into the Alps. Two great rivers cross this part of the country – the Danube and the Rhine. Berlin, the capital, is in the northeast of Germany. The far north has a bustling harbour at Hamburg, and rolling dunes and sandy beaches all along the coastlines of the North and Baltic seas.

### GERMAN MONEY

In Germany, the money people use is called marks and pfennigs. When you go to a bank, you'll see signs showing how much German money you can get in exchange for your own money.

NORTH SEA

BALTIC SEA

Denmark

Kiel

Hamburg

R. Weser

R. Elbe

Bremen

Hanover

Berlin

R. Rhine

Dresden

Frankfurt

GERMANY

Czech Republic

Black Forest

R. Danube

France

ALPS

ALPS

Munich

Switzerland

Austria

7

# In a German town

The buildings in many German towns are hundreds of years old. At the heart of most towns is a main square with a clock tower. Here, there may also be a few market stalls or kiosks selling hot snacks. Often, too, there are outdoor cafés where people stop for coffee or a glass of beer.

①

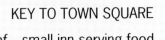

## KEY TO TOWN SQUARE

1. *Gasthof* – small inn serving food
2. *Kirche* – town church or cathedral
3. *Bäckerci* – bakery selling bread and rolls
4. *Spielwarengeschäft* – toyshop
5. *Zeitungsstand* – newsagent
6. *Postamt* – post office

9

# Going shopping

German shops open early, usually at 8 or 9 am, and stay open to 6 pm. They close about midday on Saturdays.

Toyshops are wonderful places to visit. They stock hundreds of brightly painted toy trains, cars, planes, and even model castles and villages which are perfect in every detail. Many shops also sell small cuckoo clocks that you can put together yourself.

*Torte*
(cream-cake)

*Pralinen*
(chocolates)

*Obsttorte*
(fruit tart)

*Liebkuchen*
(biscuits)

*Bonbons*
(sweets)

A *Konditorei* (pastry shop) sells all sorts of delicious cream-cakes and tarts, and also biscuits, sweets and chocolates.

11

# Eating and drinking

Two things Germany is famous for are *Sauerkraut* (pickled cabbage) and beer. But there are also dozens of breads, from crusty white to dark rye, and more kinds of sausage than days in the year. Many dishes are named after their region — frankfurters are from Frankfurt, and *Schwarzwaldtorte* is a delicious cherry and chocolate cake from the Black Forest.

Pretzels are salty snacks, nibbled with a tankard of refreshing ice-cold beer.

*Kartoffelpuffer* are fried potato cakes, often eaten with home-made apple sauce.

# KARTOFFELPUFFER

Ask a grown-up to help you cook these potato cakes. You'll need:

500 g potatoes
½ onion
1 egg
15 g flour
1 tsp salt

**1** Peel and grate the potatoes and finely chop the onion. Mix in the salt, egg and flour.
**2** Put a spoonful of the mixture into hot fat, flatten it into a pancake, and fry it until golden brown on both sides.

# Things to see and do

The northern town of Hamelin is famous for its Pied Piper. The story goes that the Piper was asked to clear the town of rats, but when he wasn't paid he led the children away with his enchanted flute. Today the story is remembered with a festival   there are even little rat sweets to nibble on!

Every Sunday during the summer, an actor dresses up as the Piper and tootles his flute in Hamelin town square.

Children dressed in rat costumes follow after him. The action all takes place on a stage outside the town hall.

The eastern town of Meissen is where porcelain was first made in Europe. You can visit the factory to watch china being hand-painted.

## PAINT YOUR OWN CHINA

Here's how to turn a plain china plate into a stunning creation of your own. You'll need a white china plate, a chinagraph pencil and ceramic paints (from an art shop), as well as paintbrushes and white spirit.

**1** Draw the pattern or picture you want on paper first, then copy it on to the plate with the pencil.

**2** Paint your pattern, then leave it to dry. (Clean off the brushes in white spirit after you finish.)

# The Black Forest

This region of wild woods and valleys in southwest Germany is where many people go on walking holidays in summer, and cross-country skiing in winter. The area is also famous for its cuckoo clocks. If you go to the town of Furtwangen, you can visit a museum with one of the most amazing clock collections in the world.

Wild boar and deer make their homes in some of the quieter corners of the Black Forest region.

# Castle country

Princes and robber barons who lived along the Rhine valley often built themselves castles on rocky hilltops, from which they plundered the country roundabout. Today, many of these castles are in ruins, although some are still open to visitors.

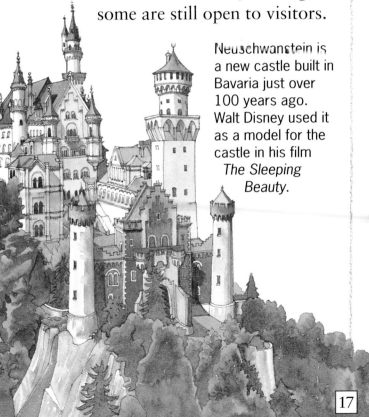

Neuschwanstein is a new castle built in Bavaria just over 100 years ago. Walt Disney used it as a model for the castle in his film *The Sleeping Beauty*.

# Two great cities

Germany has many great cities, but two that most visitors try to see are Berlin, the capital, and Munich.

The heart of Munich is the square called Marienplatz. On one side is a large town hall and clock tower.

As the Marienplatz clock strikes, its statues of dancers, musicians and jousting knights perform.

The Brandenburg Gate is a great landmark in the middle of Berlin. It was built by a German king, over 200 years ago.

### CHARLOTTENBURG PALACE

A high clock tower rises over this vast palace built in Berlin in the late 1600s. The rooms are richly decorated, and nowadays you can visit the magnificent royal apartments where the kings and queens of Germany once lived.

19

# Travelling around

**G**ermany is criss-crossed by busy motorways and ultra-fast express trains. In crowded cities, underground trains or trams are often used to get around the heavy traffic. Out in the countryside, good roads make it easy to drive just about anywhere.

Special mountain trains run up into the Alps in the south of the country. They can climb steep tracks and cope with deep snowdrifts.

△ Electric trams run in
big cities. They run on
special tracks where
other traffic can't go.

▽ A German motorway
is called an *Autobahn*.
Though wide, roads can
be choked with traffic.

# Sports and games

The three great sports in Germany are skiing, tennis and football. The Germans are keen supporters of their national football team, which has won the World Cup several times.

Many schools teach football, tennis and swimming in the afternoon. At half-term, the entire class may go to the mountains to walk or ski – downhill and cross-country are popular.

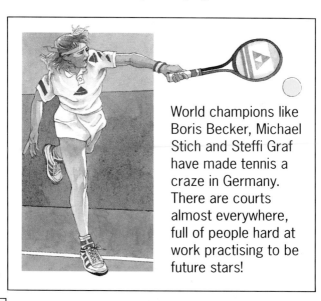

World champions like Boris Becker, Michael Stich and Steffi Graf have made tennis a craze in Germany. There are courts almost everywhere, full of people hard at work practising to be future stars!

Hang-gliding and para-gliding are popular sports in hilly country. Both make use of rising winds to soar and glide over the land.

There are enough footpaths in Germany to go three times round the world. People can be found taking long walks in forests and mountains at any time of the year.

23

# School and holidays

S chool starts early in Germany.
By 8 am, students are all sitting in
class. Soon after 1 pm, school finishes
and everyone goes home for a big
lunch. In the afternoon, students do
homework, or return to school for
sports or music lessons.

On the day they first start school,
at six years old, children are given a
big paper cone stuffed with sweets
and little toys as a treat.

Many people go to the seaside in summer. The wind is strong on the North Sea coast, so people hire beach baskets to sunbathe in comfort.

## PLAY RING-BALL

Chalk a big ring, about 8 metres wide, on the ground. Set a box in the middle, with one player to guard it. Everyone else forms a ring around the box.

The ring players have to hit the box with a thrown football, while the player in the middle keeps the ball away. Whoever hits the box is next in the middle.

# Celebrations

German children are lucky. They have two chances to get presents at Christmas. The night before 6th December, Saint Nicholas fills the shoes of good children with gifts of fruit, nuts and small toys.

A few days later, on Christmas Eve itself, everybody finds piles of presents under the Christmas tree.

In October, a great beer festival is held in Munich, bringing thousands of people into the city. Many dress in the traditional clothes of the region, which is known as Bavaria.

Christmas trees in German homes are always decorated with candles – either real or electric ones. Lots of pretty decorations are hung on the boughs, and sometimes even small chocolates.

## EASTER EGGS

In Germany, the Easter Bunny hides brightly coloured eggs in the garden for children to find! You can decorate Easter eggs, too. All you need is:

White eggs
Onion skins
  (for yellow)
Beetroot (red)
Spinach (green)
Poster paints

**1** Dye an egg by hardboiling it with a vegetable.
**2** As soon as the egg cools, you can paint it.

# Let's speak German!

NUMBERS

| | |
|---|---|
| **1** | eins |
| **2** | zwei |
| **3** | drei |
| **4** | vier |
| **5** | fünf |
| **6** | sechs |
| **7** | sieben |
| **8** | acht |
| **9** | neun |
| **10** | zehn |

*Guten Morgen*
Good morning

*Bitte*
Please

*Danke*
Thank you

*Ich möchte gern ein Eis, bitte.*
I'd like an ice-cream, please.
*Was kostet das?*
How much is it?

*Sprichst du Englisch?*
Do you speak English?

*Nein*
No

*Ja*
Yes

# Index